Khmer New Year

Time to Celebrate

It is New Year.

We will see the temple.

It is New Year.

We will go to the temple.

5

It is New Year.

We will see the star lanterns.

It is New Year.

We will have sack races.

It is New Year.

We will see the dancers.

It is New Year.

We will see the elephants.

It is New Year.

We will see the decoration.

It is New Year.

We will have fun!